IØ168Ø41

Dedicated To
Cary, Megan, Shawn and Dylan
Thank you so much for being
Patient with me
and all of my experiments.
I Love You ☺

No Dairy Diva
Written By Heather Strachan
Photographs by Heather Strachan
Edited By Karen Moncur
Assisted by Bonnie Pitchko
First Edition Printing: May 2012
St. Catharines
Second Edition Printing: September 2012
St. Catharines
Book Cover Design by Christie Hoeksema
Web Design by Future Access Inc.
Website: NoDairyDiva.com
Email: Heather@nodairydiva
www.facebook.com/NoDairyDiva

ISBN: 978-0-9881670-0-1

Table of Contents

In this first book I included the recipes that helped me curb those "Creamy Cravings". I hope this helps everyone who misses those yummy treats just like I did.

Happy Eating!!

Heather

My Story

I sat at my kitchen table with my laptop ready to go, coffee cup full and kids still in bed. Everything seemed perfect to start telling you my story.

At the age of 42, I was working full time at a job I loved, volunteering at schools, a hockey mom and trying to be the super parent we all strive to become. I worried about everyone else but myself. Then I started to get tired and feeling worn out. I couldn't do as much as I used to. I was feeling uncomfortable in my own skin from all the bloating and constipation I was starting to experience. Needless to say, I was getting worn out and did not understand why I wasn't feeling like myself.

The day I went home sick from work was difficult and I knew I had to do something to figure out what was going on inside my body. The doctors didn't really seem to help, so it was up to me. I realized through trial and error that my problem was food, mainly dairy.

I ended up eating nothing but salads and drinking coffee. I quickly lost fifteen pounds, however I could feel myself losing strength and muscle mass. Little did I know my life was going to change, without my permission. The job I enjoyed, which gave me solace from my crazy home life, had to go. The foods I loved (Lindor Truffles, for example) were no longer an option to settle that chocolate craving. I needed to do something to improve my quality of life as well as my family's. I was starting to become "not so pleasant to live with" if you know what I mean.

3

Going to a restaurant was no fun either. Imagine me sitting at the table with my cup of black coffee and dry green salad when my friends or family are enjoying a pizza or a chicken and rib platter. Even being invited to someone's home for dinner gave me anxiety. I wondered if they truly understood the gravity of my intolerance. Will they be sensitive enough to prepare something that I can eat? Do I bring my own food, trust the chef or just decline the invitation?

My intolerance does not stop at lactose. I am not able to digest anything that is dairy-based. This includes additives or preservatives.

Now I know how difficult it is to find substitutes to satisfy not only my cravings, but also my hunger. Then I thought what it must be like to have a child with severe food intolerances. My heart truly goes out to those families dealing with this issue.

While trying to find food I could eat, or cookbooks that I could learn from, I found a lot of Gluten Free, Lactose Free and Nut Free recipe books, but not a lot of complete Dairy Free without going to a vegan lifestyle. I also wanted a cookbook that I could understand with recipes that made sense when feeding a busy family with different food wants and likes, without cooking multiple meals every night.

When I decided to share my story and recipes with you, I made sure the final product was kid and family tested. I tried to create recipes that everyone could enjoy without feeling left out or simply hungry at the end of the meal.

This is my answer to the cookbook I wished I could find.

DAIRY OR

Not)))

I know this can be
really scary!!

Learning what dairy looks like on an ingredients label can be very confusing. Even when you try to find the information online, it is not always clear. I have taken the time to go through my kitchen cupboards and look up all of the questionable ingredients that tend to be confusing. Here is a list with a quick description to let you know what the ingredient actually is.

5

These are definitely dairy ingredients:

Beta-lacoglobulin

Casein

Hydrolyzed Casein

Rennet Casein

Caseinate and anything with

Caseinate (ammonium caseinate,

magnesium caseinate, potassium

caseinate and sodium caseinate)

Dry milk,

Milk solids

Modified milk ingredients,

Milk derivative

Lactalbumin and Lactalbumin

Phosphate

Lactose

Lactoferrin

Lactoglobulin

Delactosed or Demineralized Whey

Whey

Whey protein concentrate

These are <u>NOT</u> dairy ingredients even though they sound like it:

Calcium
A metallic element used in dairy products but is not dairy itself

Calcium Carbide-a grey crystalline compound

Calcium Carbonate- a natural mineral you would find in limestone, bones, and teeth and will also see it in your vitamins- it's ok

Calcium Chloride- this is a mixture of calcium and chlorine- none of which is dairy, but can be used as preservative

Calcium Disodium EDTA- this is not dairy based but from what I've read it is something you do not want too much of.

Calcium Hydroxide- colorless crystal or white powder produced by mixing calcium oxide ("lime") with water

D-Calcium Pantothenate- this is actually vitamin B5

Ingredients I like to keep on hand

These are some items I always make sure I have in my pantry or fridge, so when I have a craving or the need to experiment on a whim, I'm set.

Agave- A natural syrup in a light or dark version made from the Agave Plant- try this on pancakes or your favourite desserts.
Basmati Rice
Carob Root Chips
Cinnamon
Cocoa Powder
Fresh Pepper
Pasta
Nutmeg
Silken Tofu-Firm or Soft
Almond, Coconut or Soy Yogurt
Stewed Tomatoes
Tomato Paste
Vegan Parmesan Cheese
Corn Starch-for thickening
Vanilla, Original and Unsweetened Almond, Soy or Rice milk
Oils- Olive or Vegetable especially
Vinegars- Balsamic, Cider, Red Wine
Non Dairy Margarine
Favourite Spices
Flour and Yeast for Breads
Icing Sugar
Mayonnaise
Dark Brown Sugar
Variety of Extracts

What did the Carrot say to the Tomato?

Nothing, Veggies don't talk☺!!

Soups
And
Salads

Canadian Measurements

Casserole Sizes

1 qt.	5 cups
1 ½ qt.	7 ½ cups
2 qt.	10 cups

Oven Temperatures

F°	C°
300°	150°
325°	160°
350°	175°
375°	190°
400°	205°
425°	220°
450°	230°
475°	240°
500°	260°

Cups

¼ cup	4 tbsp.	60 ml
1/3 cup	5 1/3 tbsp.	75 ml
½ cup	8 tbsp.	125 ml
¾ cup	12 tbsp.	175 ml
1 cup	16 tbsp.	250ml

Measuring Spoons

1/8 tsp.	.5ml
¼ tsp.	1ml
½ tsp.	2ml
1 tsp.	5ml
2 tsp.	10ml
1 tbsp.	15ml

Pans

8x8 inch	20x20 cm
9x9 inch	22x22 cm
9x13 inch	22x23 cm
8x4x3 inch	20x10x7.5 cm
9x5x4 inch	22x12.5x7.5cm

Gluten Free, Egg Free, Nut Free

Mom's 5 Cup Salad

A favourite in house while I was growing up, was the 5 Cup Salad, so this was a must to re-invent. Keep the tradition alive!

  1 cup pineapple tidbits (drained)
  1 cup mandarin oranges (drained)
  1 cup shredded coconut
  1 cup mini marshmallows
    1 cup vanilla flavoured almond, soy, rice, or coconut yogurt

I like to let the pineapples and mandarins sit for 15 minutes in a strainer so they are thoroughly drained. Combine all ingredients in a medium sized bowl and keep chilled until ready to serve. Try using coloured coconut and marshmallows.

Photo on page 19

Spinach Dip

This Spinach Dip with Coconut Yogurt was awarded 2 thumbs up from my youngest son!!
This Spinach Dip with Coconut Yogurt is 2 thumbs rom my youngest son!!

1-300 g package of frozen chopped spinach
½ cup mayonnaise
¾ cup plain coconut yogurt
1 tsp. dill weed
1 tsp. minced onion
½ tsp. onion powder
¼ tsp. salt
¼ tsp. lemon
Combine all ingredients in a medium sized bowl. Serve with veggies, tortillas or pumpernickel bread.
Egg Free and Vegan Option- Switch up Mayonnaise for Vegenaise Dressing (found in refrigerated health food aisle)

Photo on page 19

Gluten Free, Egg Free, Nut Free, Vegan

Creamy Vegetable Soup

During a cold spring day I was craving a creamy soup. This was a one shot recipe. I thought it up and no tweeks were needed. What do you think?

1 tbsp. non-dairy margarine
1 tbsp. cornstarch
1 cup unsweetened almond, soy or rice milk
1 cup vegetable broth
1 cup of your favourite diced vegetables (I use carrots, corn, broccoli and cauliflower)
Salt and pepper to taste

In a small saucepan, bring vegetable broth to a boil and add diced vegetables. Cook until vegetables are slightly soft when pricked with fork. While vegetables are cooking, in another small saucepan, melt margarine then whisk flour into margarine until thick yet smooth. Slowly add milk in thirds, whisking after each addition, making sure there are no lumps. Once all milk is added, allow soup to simmer until thickened. Add vegetable broth with cooked vegetables to white sauce and simmer on low for 2-3 minutes. Add salt and pepper to taste. Makes 4 -1/2 cup servings.

Photo on page 20

13

Caesar Salad

My Daughter is dairy intolerant as well and she LOVES Caesar Salad. Mom to the Rescue!! Now she can enjoy dairy free Caesar Salad with dairy free croutons.

¼ cup plain coconut yogurt
¼ cup mayonnaise
1 tsp. vegan parmesan
1 tsp. garlic powder
1 tsp. Dijon mustard
2 tsp. lemon juice
¼ tsp. Worcestershire sauce
¼ tsp. pepper
1/8 tsp. anchovy paste (optional)
Salt, pepper and vegan parmesan to taste

Combine all ingredients in a small bowl. Gently mix preferred amount with washed and dried romaine lettuce.

Croutons (Bread recipe on page 52)
4 cups bread (diced into 1/4 pieces)
¼ cup olive oil
½ tbsp. Italian seasoning

14

½ tbsp. vegan parmesan
Preheat oven to 450°

Spread bread pieces in a single layer in a large casserole dish. Add remaining ingredients and mix thoroughly. Bake for 15-20 minutes stirring frequently.
Egg Free and Vegan Option- Change the Mayonnaise to Vegenaise Dressing
                              Photo on page 19

Greek Salad

Try this Easy New Twist on an Old Classic.

Prepare your favourite bite size macaroni; I like to use rotini or shells. These noodles tend to hold the dressing. This salad does need precise measurements of macaroni or added diced veggies. Basically you can add as much or as little as you like. Here are some veggie ideas: Tomatoes (diced or cherry), Cucumbers, Olives, Zucchini, Baby Spinach.

Dairy Free Feta

¼ cup extra firm silken tofu

2 tbsp. prepared dressing (see above)

Allow tofu to sit in a small bowl on some paper towel for about 30 minutes so excess moisture can absorb into paper towel. Remove paper towel and add prepared dressing. Use your fingers to work dressing into tofu until it is a crumbly texture.

Dressing

¾ cup olive oil

1 cup red wine vinegar

2 tsp. garlic powder

16

2 tsp. oregano

2 tsp. basil

1 ½ tsp. onion powder

2 tsp. Dijon Mustard

¾ tsp. salt

1 tsp. pepper

Combine all ingredients in a container with a lid and shake. This can keep in refrigerator for 3 days.

Gluten Free and Vegan Option

Trade up the Macaroni for your favourite gluten free or vegan option

Once you have dressing, feta, macaroni and veggies combine to your customized salad and enjoy!

Photo on page 20

Pumpkin Soup

Fantastic for the Pumpkin Lover.
Smooth and Scrumptious!!

1 cup pumpkin puree

1 1/3 cup vegetable broth or stock

3 tsp. pumpkin pie spice

4 tsp. blonde agave

¼ tsp. salt and pepper (or to taste)

In a medium saucepan, combine all ingredients and bring to boil then simmer on low for 10 min.

Makes approximately 4- ½ cup servings.

Photo on page 20

Spinach Dip
Page 12

Mom's 5
Cup
Salad
Page 11

Caesar Salad
Page 14

Greek Salad
Page 17

Pumpkin
Soup
Page 18

Creamy
Vegetable Soup
Page 13

Side
Dishes

These recipes should
help with those
Comfort Food
Cravings.

Scalloped Potatoes

6 potatoes peeled and thinly sliced
1 cooking onion diced
2 tbsp. oil
2 cups and 2 tbsp. unsweetened almond, soy or rice milk
2 tbsp. cornstarch
1 tsp. parsley
1/8 tsp. celery salt

½ tsp. pepper
½ tsp. salt
¼ tsp. garlic powder
¼ cup diced spinach (optional)
¼ cup dairy free bread crumbs (optional)

Preheat oven to 375 °.

Place sliced potatoes in a greased casserole dish. Preheat non-stick frying pan with the oil then add the onions. Slowly cook the

onions until clear. In a separate small container combine cornstarch with milk (I use a small covered Tupperware bowl to shake until there are no clumps), then add to onions. Reduce heat and stir constantly. While stirring, add spices. Continue to heat milk until it is the thickness of a cream soup. Before pouring over potatoes, add spinach if you desire. Sprinkle bread crumbs over mixture. Cover dish and bake for 45-50 min. Potatoes should be tender when pricked with fork. Uncover and broil on high for 15 min or until top is lightly browned. Allow to sit for 5-10 min before serving. Makes approximately 6-½ cup servings.

This was tough to re-create, but it is a wonderful recipe and no one will know the difference.

Photo on page 31

Gluten Free, Egg Free, Nut Free, Vegan

Alfredo Sauce
And Your Favourite Pasta

This sauce was a definite must re-invent.
It's my daughter's favourite.

4 tbsp. non-dairy margarine
4 tbsp. cornstarch
2 2/3 cup unsweetened
almond, soy or rice milk
1 tbsp. Italian seasoning
1 ½ tsp. garlic powder
1 tsp. onion powder
¼ tsp. salt
½ tsp. pepper
1/8 tsp. nutmeg
1 tbsp. vegan parmesan

In a medium size saucepan,
melt margarine over
medium heat until soft, then
whisk in flour until smooth and slightly
bubbly. Add first portion of milk and whisk
until smooth. Once that starts to thicken, add
second milk portion. Whisk this frequently
until thickened, while adding spices. Once
this has thickened, add 1/3 portion and
continue heating and whisking until sauce is

at your desired consistency. Add salt and fresh ground pepper to taste. Makes approximately 6 half cup portions of sauce. Pour over your favourite pasta and enjoy.

This can be kept
in fridge
for a day or two.
You may need
to add
your choice
of milk
to thin sauce while
re-heating.

Photo on page 32

Gluten Free, Egg Free, Nut Free, Vegan

Mashed Potatoes and Gravy

I prefer to use yellow potatoes
when making mashed potatoes.
I find the flavour is a little smoother

6-8 medium potatoes
¼ cup non-dairy margarine

Peel and boil potatoes until potatoes are soft when poked with a fork. Drain potato water into a large bowl and set water aside. You will use this later. Mash potatoes using margarine and potato water. Only use approximately ¼ cup potato water as you want to have firm mashed potatoes. The amount of potato water will depend on the type of potato as well. Remember you can always add water, but it's really hard to take it back out.

Gravy

2 tbsp. canola oil
2 tbsp. cornstarch
1 1/3 cup vegetable, beef or chicken broth
½ cup potato water
¼ tsp. soy sauce
½-1 tsp. Montreal chicken or steak Spice (adjust according to your preference)

In a small saucepan melt margarine, then whisk in flour. Whisk constantly over medium heat until the margarine and flour start to turn brown. Be careful, do not burn. Slowly add broth while continuing to whisk. Then add remaining ingredients and bring to boil, then reduce heat and simmer on low for 5-7 minutes.

Photo on page 31

Gluten, Egg and Vegan Options, Nut Free

Macaroni and Cheese

This is what I missed the most. I knew I hit the jackpot when my teenage son went in for the second plate full. A must try. There is no substitute for the taste of real cheese. However, the combination of the spices used gives you a different, yet yummy flavour.

¼ cup non-dairy margarine

¼ cup cornstarch

2 2/3 cup unsweetened almond, rice or soy milk (divided into 3 portions)

1 tsp. sugar

1 tsp. mustard powder

1 tsp. turmeric

2 tsp. flaked nutritional yeast

¼ tsp. salt

¼ tsp. onion powder

¼ tsp. garlic powder

¼ tsp. pepper

2 tbsp. ketchup (use more if you like)

375 ml box of elbow macaroni

Preheat oven to 375 °. Lightly grease a 2 L baking dish. Set aside. In a large saucepan, prepare the elbow noodles to al dente. Drain and rinse the macaroni and return to large saucepan. In a medium saucepan, begin to melt non-dairy margarine. Add flour to margarine and whisk until there are no lumps. Add first portion of almond milk, while whisking constantly. Once this has thickened, add second portion of almond milk while whisking. Add spices at this point, while whisking, making sure there are no lumps or clumps.

Once this has thickened, add last portion of milk and whisk frequently while this is thickening. Add ketchup. Let simmer for 3-5min, but do not thicken too much. Pour this mixture over elbow noodles and stir thoroughly. Place your mac and cheese into prepared baking dish and bake covered for 15-20 minutes, then remove cover and broil macaroni and cheese on high for 5-10 minutes for a golden top.

Gluten Free, Egg Free and Vegan Option

Trade up the macaroni for your
favourite gluten free, egg free
Photo on page 32

Rose' Sauce

This is a wonderful switch from your basic tomato sauce. A very nice lunch time treat!!

2 tbsp. olive oil

2 tbsp. cornstarch

1½ cup unsweetened almond, soy or rice milk (in 3 portions)

Pinch of nutmeg

1 tsp. Italian seasoning

1 tsp. garlic powder

1 tsp. onion powder

½ tsp. basil

1/8 tsp. salt

¾ tsp. pepper

1 tbsp. vegan parmesan

1-796 ml can of stewed tomatoes (blended)

In a medium sized saucepan, heat olive oil then whisk in flour until smooth and bubbly. Pour in first portion of milk then whisk until blended. Add second portion of milk and whisk until blended and heat until mixture thickens. Then once the final portion of milk is blended, add remaining ingredients. Simmer on low for 15-20 minutes. Top your favourite pasta with sauce and garnish with a pinch of parsley.   Photo on page 32

30

Mashed Potatoes and Gravy
Page 26

Scalloped Potatoes
Page 22

Alfredo
Sauce
Page 24

Rose'
Sauce
Page 30

Macaroni
And Cheese
Page 28

When you
think
outside
the box
anything is
POSSIBLE!

No Dairy Entrées

Gluten Free, Egg Free, Nut Free and Vegan Option

Shepherd's Pie

I actually have 2 great Shepherd's Pie recipes
so I gave you both as well as the
Vegan Option.   Photo on 45

Shepherd's Pie with Gravy

This recipe has multiple steps that can
be done at the same time so read full
recipe first then let's get started.
Preheat oven to 400°.

Ground Beef, Chicken or Pork

1 pound ground beef, chicken or pork
1 cooking onion (diced)
2-3 tsp. Montreal Steak Spice or Chicken Spice (adjust
according to personal preference)
½ cup prepared gravy
Preheat frying pan and fry ground beef with the
onions. Drain grease from ground beef. Add
Montreal Steak Spice and gravy. Place ground beef in
bottom of 2L.

Mashed Potatoes

6-8 medium potatoes
¼ cup non-dairy margarine
Peel and boil potatoes until potatoes are soft when
poked with a fork. Drain potato water into a large
bowl and set water aside. You will use this later.

Mash potatoes using margarine and potato water. Only use ¼ cup to 1/3 cup potato water as you want to have firm mashed potatoes.

Gravy

2 tbsp. non-dairy margarine
2 tbsp. cornstarch
1 1/3 cup vegetable, beef or chicken broth
½ cup potato water
¼ tsp. soy sauce
¼ tsp. Montreal Chicken or Steak spice

In a small saucepan, melt margarine then whisk in flour. Whisk constantly over medium heat until the margarine and flour start to turn brown. Be careful, do not burn. Slowly add broth while continuing to whisk. Then add remaining ingredients and bring to boil then reduce heat and simmer on low for 5-7 minutes.

Shepherd's Pie Preparation

2 cups corn (cooked)
2 tbsp. non dairy margarine
In the bottom of a 2L casserole dish evenly spread around beef, chicken, pork or vegetarian option. Then drain and spoon corn over first layer. Finally, carefully spoon then spread mashed potatoes over corn then spread margarine over potatoes. This will allow potatoes to brown nicely while baking. Cover and bake for 40-45 minutes. Then remove cover and broil on high for 5- 10 minutes. Makes 6-8 servings.

Shepherd's Pie with Creamed Corn

This recipe has multiple steps that can be done at the same time so read full recipe first then let's get started. Preheat oven to 400°.

Mashed Potatoes

6-8 medium potatoes
¼ cup non-dairy margarine

Peel and boil potatoes until potatoes are soft when poked with a fork. Drain potato water into a large bowl and set water aside. You will use this later. Mash potatoes using margarine and potato water. Only use ¼ cup to 1/3 cup potato water as you want to have firm mashed potatoes.

Ground Beef, Chicken or Pork

1 pound ground beef, chicken or pork
1 cooking onion (diced)
1 tsp. Montreal Steak or Chicken Spice
1-398ml can of creamed corn
Preheat frying pan and fry ground beef with the onions.
Drain grease from ground beef. Add Montreal Steak Spice
and creamed corn.

Shepherd's Pie Preparation

2 tbsp. non dairy margarine
Place ground beef in bottom of 2L casserole dish. Gently
and evenly spoon mashed potatoes over meat and corn
mixture. I like to spread non-dairy margarine over the top
of the potatoes which will help them brown easier. Cover
and bake for 40-45 minutes then remove cover and broil on
high for 5- 10 minutes to brown top. Allow to sit for 5
minutes before serving. Makes 6-8 servings.

I made all three recipes one day and my kids actually preferred the Vegan Option. (I wasn't going to tell them it was mushroom. "They don't like mushrooms." lol)

Gluten Free, Egg Free, Nut Free

Vegan Shepherd's Pie

1L Casserole

2 tbsp. vegetable oil
8 ounces of mushrooms (finely chopped)
1 cooking onion (diced)
½ -1 tsp. Montreal Steak Spice or Chicken Spice (adjust according to personal preference)
¼ cup prepared gravy
1 cup cooked corn
2 cups prepared mashed potatoes
1 tbsp. non-dairy margarine

Preheat oven to 400°

Preheat frying pan with oil then slowly sauté onions and mushrooms over medium heat. Make sure not to burn them. Mushrooms will turn a dark brown colour. Add steak/chicken spice and prepared gravy. Continue to sauté on medium low until mushrooms mixture has thickened. Spread in bottom of greased casserole dish. Top with 1 cup of cooked corn, then spoon mashed potatoes carefully over corn. Finally spread margarine over potatoes and bake for 20 minutes then broil for 5-10 minutes or until brown.

Egg Free, Nut Free and Vegan
Pizza Dough
Makes 2-4 Pizzas

I am told this pizza dough is the best pizza dough ever. Guess who is the new family Super Hero!!

1 cup warm/hot water

1 tbsp. instant yeast

1 tbsp. sugar

2 tbsp. olive oil

2 cups and 2 tbsp. flour

1 tsp. salt

1 tbsp. ground flax (optional)

In a large bowl, dissolve yeast and sugar into the water and allow proofing for 10 minutes. (If your mixture does not rise and bubble then your yeast is dead) Combine salt, olive oil and ground flax to yeast mixture. Add flour 1 cup at a time. Once mixture is too thick to stir, knead remainder of flour into large dough ball. Place dough into well oiled bowl and turn dough ball over in bowl until all of dough is covered in oil. Allow to rise for 1 hour with warm damp cloth covering bowl. Once dough has risen to at least twice its original size cut dough in half with oiled knife. Place dough on clean surface or parchment paper dusted with flour. Shape dough and add toppings. Bake in preheated 425° oven for 15 to 20 minutes. Pizza is ready when bottom is light brown.

Pizza dough can be kept in freezer for future use.

Photo on page 46

Nut Free with Gluten Free, Egg Free and Vegan Options

Lasagna

This recipe will make a 9x9 inch Lasagna with Marinara sauce to spare. There are several steps to this, but well worth it. So take the day and enjoy. It is even better the second day. This recipe has multiple steps that can be done at the same time, so read the full recipe first then let's get started.

Photo on page 46

Chunky Marinara Sauce

1/4 cup olive oil
½ sweet onions (diced)
1 garlic clove (peeled and diced)
2- 796 ml cans of stewed tomatoes
1-196 ml can of tomato paste
1 tbsp. Vegan Parmesan
½ tsp. oregano
½ tsp. basil
¼ tsp. salt
½ tsp. pepper
½ tsp. sugar

In a stewing pot preheat the oil then add the onions and garlic. Sauté garlic and onions on medium until onions are clear (do not burn the garlic). Add remaining ingredients and bring to boil, then reduce heat to low and simmer for 2-3 hours. Stir occasionally.

Ground Beef, Pork or Chicken

1 pound ground beef, chicken or pork
In a large frying pan brown your choice of ground beef, pork or chicken. When done add 1 cup of Marina sauce and simmer on low for 5 minutes. Set aside

Lasagna Noodles

In a large sauce pan bring water to boil then add 12 noodles. Boil until al dente. Drain and rinse under cold water. Set aside

White Sauce

¼ cup olive oil
1/3 cup cornstarch
2 2/3 cups unsweetened almond, soy or rice milk (divided into 3 portions)
1 tbsp. Italian seasoning
2 tbsp. vegan parmesan cheese
1 ½ tsp. garlic powder
1 tsp. onion powder
¼ tsp. salt
½ tsp. pepper
1/8 tsp. nutmeg
In a medium size saucepan, heat oil then add flour and whisk thoroughly at a simmer until there are no lumps. Add first portion of milk and whisk until blended. Add second portion and whisk. Allow to thicken then add final portion of milk and all spices.

Turn Page

Continue to simmer on low for 10 minutes. You will want consistency of sauce to be thick enough to coat the back of a spoon.

Gluten, Egg, Vegetarian and Vegan Options

2 cups of diced fresh vegetables instead of meat

In a large non-stick frying pan warm 2 cups of diced vegetables and add 1 cup of marina sauce. Simmer on low for 2-3 minutes.

Also change your lasagna noodles to gluten or egg free favourite.

Preheat oven to 400°.

Preparation

Once you have your marinara sauce, white sauce, meat or vegetable sauce and lasagna noodles ready, it is time to layer. Start by spreading a thin layer of marina sauce first then a layer of 3 noodles. Make sure the noodles do not overlap each other. Add a layer of white sauce that would be about ¼ cm thick followed by ½ of the meat/vegetable sauce. Next add a layer of 3 noodles, then add about ½ cm -3/4 cm of white sauce. Then, add another layer of noodles and remaining meat/vegetable sauce. Finally, add last layer of noodles then thin layer of white sauce and thin layer of marina sauce. Bake uncovered for 30 minutes, then broil on high for 10 minutes. Allow lasagna to sit for 20 minutes before serving.

Gluten Free, Egg Free, Nut Free with Vegan Option

Creamy Chicken Stew

If you're not sure what to do with your leftover chicken or turkey, this is something different from the Hot Sandwich.

2 cups vegetable or chicken broth
2 cups chopped vegetables (fresh or frozen)
½ tsp. rosemary
½ tsp. minced onion
½ tsp. garlic powder
6 medium cooked, diced potatoes
2 cups cooked diced chicken
¼ cup non-dairy margarine
¼ cup cornstarch
2 cups unsweetened almond, soy or rice milk
Salt and pepper to taste

43

For this recipe, you will need a small and a medium size saucepan. In the small saucepan bring broth, vegetables and spices to a boil then reduce heat and let simmer for 3-4 minutes. In the medium saucepan, melt the margarine, then whisk the flour into the melted margarine until smooth. Slowly add the milk in thirds, whisking until smooth after each addition of milk.
Stir the broth, vegetables, potatoes, chicken, salt and pepper into the milk mixture. Reduce heat and let simmer on low for 10-15 minutes. This makes approximately 5-6 one cup portions.

Vegan Option : Simply leave out the chicken or turkey and use organic vegetable broth.

Photo on page 45

Shepherd's Pie Page 34

Creamy Chicken Stew Page 43

Lasagna Page 40

Pizza
Dough
Page 39

Breads,

Cookies

and

Muffins

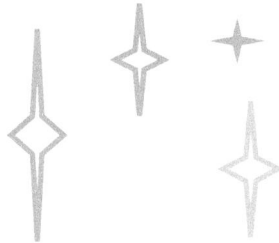

Nut Free

Apple Cranberry Bread

This easy recipe can pretty much be made from the ingredients you probably already have around your kitchen ☺

1 cup unsweetened applesauce
½ cup sugar
½ cup brown sugar
1 cup mayonnaise
1 tsp. vanilla
2 cups flour
1 tsp. cinnamon
¾ tsp. baking soda
¾ tsp. baking powder
½ tsp. salt
1 cup dried cranberries
½ tsp. cinnamon (to sprinkle on top of bread-optional)
½ tsp. sugar (to sprinkle on top of bread-optional)

Preheat oven to 375 °. Prepare 8x8 square pan or 4x9 loaf pan with oil and dusting of flour. In a medium sized bowl mix together flour, baking soda, cinnamon, baking powder, baking soda and salt. Set aside. In another large bowl, thoroughly combine applesauce, sugar, brown sugar, vanilla and mayonnaise. Slowly add dry ingredients to applesauce mixture. Gently add cranberries. Place mixture into prepared pan and sprinkle with optional sugar and cinnamon. Bake for 45-50 minutes. Test with toothpick. Toothpick should come out dry when loaf is pricked. Cool Apple Cranberry Bread on wire rack. I prefer to leave bread out for the first day then store in an airtight container. **Photo on page 64**

Nut Free

Banana Bread

When you have those brown bananas kicking around this is a moist, yummy and easy recipe that the whole family will enjoy. Mine does!!

3 ripe medium size bananas (mashed)
1 cup mayonnaise
1 tsp. vanilla extract
1 cup brown sugar
2 cups flour
½ tsp. cinnamon
¾ tsp. baking soda
¾ tsp. baking powder
½ tsp. salt
½ tsp. cinnamon (to sprinkle on bread)
½ tsp. sugar (to sprinkle on top of bread)

Preheat oven to 375 °Prepare loaf pan with oil and flour. In a medium size bowl, stir together bananas, mayonnaise, brown sugar and vanilla. In a separate bowl, thoroughly combine dry ingredients expect for the optional sugar and cinnamon. Gently add dry ingredients to banana mixture. Only stir until completely mixed. Pour mixture evenly into prepared loaf pan and sprinkle with additional cinnamon and sugar. Bake for 45 minutes. Test with toothpick. Toothpick should come out dry when loaf is pricked. Cool Banana Bread on wire rack.

Photo on page 63

*The Apple Cranberry
Bread and Banana Bread
are
fantastic recipes to
<u>Bake and Freeze</u>.
I always make up 2 or 3
at a time and bring one
out when I need it.*

White Sandwich Bread

This is a sweet bread that can easily have the sugar reduced. If you are like me, time is of the essence. I always bake 2-4 loaves at a time and freeze. If you find you have bread that needs to be used up, cut thick slices for French Toast or freeze and save for Bread Pudding or Stuffing.

2 cups warm/hot water
2 tbsp. instant yeast
½ cup sugar (this can be reduced to ¼ cup)
1 ½ tsp. salt
¼ cup vegetable oil
2 tbsp. ground flax (optional)
5 cups all-purpose flour

Prepare two bread pans with oil and lightly powder with flour. In a large bowl dissolve yeast and sugar in to the water and allow to proof (rise) for 10 minutes. (If your mixture does not rise and bubble, then your yeast is dead) Combine salt, oil and ground flax to yeast

mixture. Add flour 1 cup at a time. Once mixture is too thick to stir, knead remainder of flour into large dough ball. Cut dough in half with oiled knife and gently remove each half from bowl and lightly oil entire half before placing into prepared pan. Now preheat oven to 350°. Let dough to rise to about 1 inch over the pan. Bake for 25 minutes on center rack. Allow bread to cool 5 minutes before removing from pan and placing on wire rack to cool.

Photo on page 64

Nut Free, Egg Free and Vegan

Cinnamon Bread with Almond Icing

My family loves cinnamon buns and it frustrated me to watch them enjoy their special treat. So I did something about it. The recipe varies a bit when making the buns to allow the buns to be a little lighter and fluffier. Do not try to use the bun recipe for the bread, I did and it just wasn't the same.

Photo on page 64

2 cups warm/hot water

2 tbsp. instant yeast

½ cup sugar

1 ½ tsp. salt

¼ cup vegetable oil

2 tbsp. ground flax (optional)

5 cups all-purpose flour

¼ - ½ cup brown sugar

1 -1 ½ tsp. cinnamon

In a large bowl, dissolve yeast and sugar into water and allow proofing for 10 minutes. (If your mixture does not rise and bubble then your yeast is dead) Combine salt, oil and ground flax to yeast mixture. Add flour 1 cup at a time. Once mixture is too thick to stir, knead remainder of flour into large dough ball. Place dough into well oiled bowl and turn dough ball

53

over in bowl until all of dough is covered in oil. Allow to rise for 1 hour with warm wet cloth covering bowl. While waiting, prepare two bread pans with oil and lightly powder with flour. Once dough has risen to at least twice its original size, cut dough in half with oiled knife and gently remove each half from bowl. Roll dough on a clean surface or parchment paper dusted with flour to about a ½ inch thickness to about a size of 8X13 inches. Sprinkle brown sugar and cinnamon evenly over bread dough making sure it is taken to the edges of dough. Tightly roll dough width wise ensuring you pinch the air out of dough while rolling it. Place into prepared loaf pans. Lightly brush with vegetable oil. Allow to rise and additional 30-45 minutes covered by a warm, damp cloth. Preheat oven to 350°. Bake for 25 minutes. Allow to cool for 5 minutes then remove bread and/or rolls from pans and cool on a wire rack.

Almond Icing

1 tbsp. vegetable oil
3 tbsp. vanilla almond milk
2 cups icing sugar
In a medium bowl, combine all ingredients and mix until smooth. Spread over rolls and/or bread.

Photo on page 64

Cinnamon Buns

Reduce sugar to ¼ cup and
flour to 4 ¼ cups.
Allow to rise as the bread.
When rolling the Cinnamon
Rolls tightly roll dough
lengthwise ensuring you
pinch the dough with each roll
to make sure there are
no air pockets. Slice into 1-1 ½
inch portions and
place in a 9x13 prepared pan 1
inch apart.
Let rise for approximately 45
min. or until buns are touching.
Bake for 15-18 minutes at 350°.

Photo on page 64

Nut Free, Egg Free and Vegan with a Sugar Free Option

Fluffy Pancakes

Everyone has those crazy weekend mornings when everything is going on and then someone says "Let's have pancakes" (usually my husband). Then they all jump on the band wagon and pancakes it is. Well this works great for them but my daughter and I can't enjoy them. This recipe is for all those people who love pancakes, but can't eat them. Not only will this satisfy you, but the whole family will have a new favourite pancake. TRUST ME!! **Photo on page 63**

1 cup flour
1/3 cup sugar
2 tbsp. baking powder
¼ cup instant soy milk
½ tsp. salt
1¼ cup water
2 tbsp. vegetable oil
1 tbsp. flax (optional)
½ tsp. cinnamon (optional)
Preheat oiled griddle to 400 °.
In a medium size bowl combine dry ingredients thoroughly, then add water and oil. Stir until there are no lumps left. Place approximately ¼ cup of pancake batter onto preheated griddle.

Allow bubbles to slightly form on top of pancake, then flip over and cook for about ½ the time it took to cook the first side. Try these pancakes with topped with fresh fruit and agave. Yum!

Sugar Free Option

Substitute the sugar for 3 tbsp. agave and I would definitely add the flax.

I like to top these pancakes with a fruit syrup. To do this I use about 1 cup of frozen fruit and add a tablespoon of agave or honey and microwave for about 2 minutes.
This makes a great fruity syrup.

Caramel Apple Pancakes

To create a great twist, once you place batter on griddle sprinkle pancake with brown sugar and cinnamon then thinly sliced apples or pears. Allow batter to bubble then carefully flip pancake over and cook for ½ the time it took you to cook the first side.

Lightly drizzle agave (for the vegan flair) or honey and this is an absolute treat.
Photo on page 63

Chocolate Chip Cheats

2/3 cup vegetable oil

2/3 cup sugar

2/3 cup brown sugar

1 tsp. vanilla

1 egg

1¼ cup flour

1 tsp. baking powder

1 tsp. baking soda

¼ tsp. salt

2/3 cup carob chips

Preheat oven to 350 °.

In a medium size bowl, beat together with mixer the oil, white and brown sugars, vanilla and egg. In separate bowl combine flour, baking soda, baking powder and salt. Blend dry ingredients into mixture until too thick to blend then stir remainder. Add carob chips. Drop dough by teaspoons

on to baking sheet 1 ½ inches apart. Bake for
7-9 minutes, or until lightly browned. Makes
approximately 2 dozen.

Egg Free and Vegan Option
 Simply substitute the egg with an egg
replacer.

Photo on page 63

This recipe can be
placed in a greased
pie plate for
**Chocolate Chip
Cookie Pie**

Nut Free with Egg Free and Vegan Options

Lemon Cranberry Cookies

If these cookies don`t taste like summer I don`t know what does. Partner them with a tall glass of lemonade or orange juice and your mouth will have no choice but to smile☺

2/3 cup vegetable oil
2/3 cup brown sugar
2/3 cup sugar
1 egg
1 ½ tsp. lemon extract
1¼ cup flour
1 tsp. baking soda
1 tsp. baking powder
¼ tsp. salt
2/3 cup dried cranberries

Preheat oven to 350°.
In a medium bowl, beat together with mixer the oil, white and brown sugars, vanilla and egg. In separate bowl combine flour, baking soda, baking powder and salt. Stir dry ingredients into blended mixture. Stir in dried cranberries. Drop teaspoon size cookie dough onto baking sheet 1 ½ inches apart. Bake for 7-9 minutes or until lightly browned. Makes approximately 2 dozen.

Egg Free and Vegan Option

Simply substitute the egg with an egg replacer.

Photo on page 63

Nut Free with Egg Free and Vegan Options

<u>My Favourit☺ Maple Cookies</u>

These cookies have the perfect combination of crunch and chew. My boys will take a bowl and eat them like potato chips if I don`t keep my eye on them.

2/3 cup vegetable oil
1 1/3 cup dark brown sugar
1 egg
1 ½ tsp. maple extract
1¼ cup flour
1 tsp. baking soda
1 tsp. baking powder
¼ tsp. salt

Preheat oven to 350°. In a medium bowl beat together with mixer the oil, brown sugar, vanilla and egg. In separate bowl combine flour, baking soda, baking powder and salt. Stir dry ingredients into blended mixture. Drop teaspoon size cookie dough onto baking sheet 1 ½ inches apart. Bake for 7-9 minutes or until lightly browned. Makes approximately 2 dozen.

<u>Egg Free and Vegan Option</u>

Simply substitute the egg with an egg replacer.

PHOTO ON PAGE 64

If your family is like mine, they can devour a plate of cookies in a matter of moments. This is my solution to make these cookies last a little longer. Bake a double or triple batch and freeze some cookies for a later date. They are just as tasty once defrosted and paired with your favourite mug of warm comfort. It will seem like you just finished baking. My go to cookie sidekick on a chilly day is warm mug of chocolate almond milk.

$\mathcal{D}$ESSERTS

Sshhh!!!

If you don't tell them, they will never know you just served a dairy free dessert ☺

Lemon Cake

I would like to introduce you to our New Birthday Cake. My family orders this cake for their birthday whether they are dairy intolerant or not.
Top this with the
" I can't believe it tastes like Cream Cheese icing" ICING   Photo on page 77

2 cups sugar
½ cup non-dairy margarine
4 eggs
3 cups flour
2 tbsp. baking powder
¼ tsp. salt
3 tsp. lemon extract
2 cups unsweetened almond, soy, or rice milk

Preheat oven to 350 ° and prepare your cake pans with oil and flour and parchment paper.
Cream together, non-dairy margarine and sugar. Add eggs one at a time, blending after each egg added.
In a second small bowl

combine your dry ingredients. In a third small bowl combine your milk and lemon extract. When combining the milk and dry ingredients to the creamed mixture, alternate between wet and dry ingredients, mixing well between each addition. Pour into prepared pan(s). Bake for 20 – 25 minutes for 2- 9 inch pans. Adjust baking time for sheet pan. Remove cake from pans once done and cool on wire racks. This recipe can easily be cut in half, if you need a smaller cake

☹ *Sorry to those who require a gluten free, sugar free, egg free or vegan recipe, but I could not bring myself to change this recipe. It is awesome as it is and deserves to stay that way. Don't worry; I will not forget about anyone, more recipes will be coming that will satisfy all.* ☺

"I can't believe this tastes like Cream Cheese Icing" ICING

½ cup non-dairy margarine (softened)
2/3 cup vanilla almond milk
(Do not substitute soy or rice milk)
2 tsp. lemon extract
½ tsp. salt
7 ½ cups icing sugar

In a medium size bowl, combine margarine, milk, lemon extract and salt. Slowly blend icing sugar into mixture eventually having to fold last remaining icing into mixture by hand.

Nut Free

Royal Icing

6 egg whites
1 tsp. cream of tartar
8 cups icing sugar

Beat egg whites until fluffy and set aside. Sift together icing sugar and cream of tartar. Slowly blend sifted icing sugar to egg whites until smooth.

I wanted to give you a choice of icing. When it comes to icing, don't be afraid to experiment with flavours or colours. Make it your own!

Pumpkin Cheese Cake

All I need to say is
"Who doesn't love <u>CHEESECAKE</u>."
This was a must re-invent in my
quest to quench those difficult
cravings!!
Photo on page 77

Preheat oven to 325 °

Crust

1 cup graham cracker
cookie crumbs,
¼ cup non-dairy margarine
¼ cup sugar

Lightly oil the bottom and
sides of 9 inch pie plate.
Melt the rest. Add sugar,
then add melted non-dairy
margarine and press
mixture into pan. Bake for
15-20 min until lightly
brown. Cool on wire rack.

Filling

2 cups silken tofu (room temperature)
2 cups pumpkin puree
3/4 cup sugar
1 tsp. vanilla
3 tbsp. lemon juice
1 tsp. ground cinnamon
1/2 tsp. ground ginger
1/2 tsp. ground cloves
1/2 tsp. ground nutmeg
1/4 tsp. salt
2 1/2 tbsp. cornstarch
3 eggs, room temperature, beaten

Beat tofu in mixer until smooth. Add sugar, mix. Add lemon juice, mix. Add pumpkin, mix. Add beaten eggs, vanilla, spices & mix. Pour into crust. Bake for 1 hour until outside is set, but inside is still a tiny bit loose. Then turn oven off and leave door slightly open and leave cheesecake in oven for another 30 minutes. Cool on wire rack until cool. Refrigerate overnight for best results

Gluten Free, Nut Free and Vegan
with Sugar Free Option
Rice Pudding

When I made this the first time my 11 year old had friends over. I asked them to test it for me. Reluctantly they agreed. I gave them each a small bowl. Well to make a long story short, they actually and literally ate the remaining amount straight from the pot and finished it all. I guessed that meant that this recipe was kid approved☺

½ cup uncooked basmati rice
(thoroughly rinsed with cold water in a colander)
2 tbsp. sugar
½ cup raisins
3 1/2 cups vanilla almond milk-separated into 3 portions
(1- 2 cup portion and 3- ½ cup portions) rice or soy milk can be substituted

In large saucepan, on medium low heat combine 2 cups milk, rice, raisins and sugar and slowly bring to boil while stirring often. When mixture begins to thicken, slowly add first ½ cup of the reserved milk. Allow to thicken again, then add second ½ cup of milk and continue through third ½ cup of milk. Once pudding is thick enough, remove from heat. This can be served warm or cold. Try adding some cinnamon or agave.

Sugar Free Option

Substitute the sugar with 1 tbsp. honey or 1 tbsp. agave (if you would like to keep it vegan)

Photo on page 78

Gluten Free, Nut Free

Chocolate Mousse

This recipe contains raw egg.

Photo on page 77
1 tbsp. non-dairy
margarine
1 cup carob root chips
1/3 cup hot water
1 tbsp. sugar
4 eggs, separated

In a double boiler, combine the margarine, carob chips, sugar and hot water and whisk constantly until the mixture has melted. While whisking constantly slowly add the egg yolk. Continue to cook for 2 minutes while whisking. Remove from heat when mixture has a smooth creamy texture. Let chocolate mixture cool on counter while you blend the egg white to a firm meringue, then fold chocolate into the meringue. Pour into dessert bowls or wine glasses for a fancy look and chill for 3 hours. Garnish and enjoy. Makes 4- ½ cup servings.

If you do not have a

double boiler,

a large metal bowl

over a pot of boilig water

will do just fine.

Sometimes it works better.

Bread
Pudding

This is fantastic warm treat on a cool day. Imagine bread pudding with a coffee, your favourite chair and a movie. Need I say more? I have also put this in a greased mini loaf pan for yummy pull apart bread.

4 cups of diced bread
¼ cup raisins
1 apple (peeled and diced)
1-250 ml can of coconut milk
2 eggs
1/3 cup brown sugar
1/3 cup sugar
¼ nutmeg
1 tsp. cinnamon

Preheat oven to 350°.
Grease a 1 L casserole dish and place in bread crumbs, apples and raisins. In a shakeable container mix the remaining ingredients and pour over bread. Gently yet thoroughly mix together then let mixture sit for 30 minutes stirring every 10 minutes so liquid can be absorbed evenly by bread. Bake for 30- 35 minutes. To check if done just separate the middle of Bread Pudding with fork. This should not be mushy but more of a cake-like texture. Drizzle with agave for a different flavour.

Almond, soy or rice milk can be substituted for the coconut milk, however I find the coconut milk gives it a lighter texture and flavour. Don`t be shy to add other fruit or nuts to make this your own.

Photo on page 78

Pumpkin
Cheesecake
Page 69

Chocolate
Mousse
Page 73

Lemon
Cake
Page 66

Rice Pudding Page 71

Bread Pudding Page 75

Index

www.ingramcontent.com/pod-product-compliance
Lightning Source LLC
Chambersburg PA
CBHW041529090426